Copyright © 2025 by Claudeen Martinez

All rights reserved.

No portion of this book may be reproduced in any form without written permission from the publisher or author, except as permitted by Australian copyright law.

Dedicated to
Sienna, Gabriel, Olivia, Lucas and Emeline,
whose love reflects the light of Heaven and reminds me
daily of God's greatest gifts .

Contents

How to use this book	5
Parents and carers guide	8
What is prayer	13
The Saints	17
Saint Mary (Mother of God)	18
Saint Joseph	20
Saint Francis of Assisi	22
Saint Therese of Lisieux	24
Saint Michael the Archangel	26
Saint Clare	28
Saint Nicholas	30
Saint Anthony of Padua	32
Saint Patrick	34
Saint Mark	36
Saint Luke	38
Saint George	40
Saint Charbel	42
Saint Ephrem	44
Saint Gregory the Illuminator	46
Saint Isaac of Nineveh	48
Saint Josephine Bakhita	50
Saint Rose of Lima	52
Saint Bridget of Sweden	54
Saint Mary MacKillop	56
The Saints Stories	58
Seeking Saintly Guidance	66
Feast Days	70
Final Message	72

How To Use This Book

Discover the magic in these pages
With stories of saints through all the ages

How To Use This Book.

Dear child, loved more than you know,
God walks beside you wherever you go.
On sunny mornings or stormy nights,
His arms are ready to hold you tight.

The saints are near, they know your name,
They walked the earth and felt the same.
They walked with courage, joy, and grace,
And now they shine from Heaven's place.

When you feel lost or filled with doubt,
Or when big feelings all rush out.
Just take this book and have a look,
There's comfort waiting in each nook.

How To Use This Book.

The prayers inside are here for you,
To help you know what's kind and true.
You'll find a saint to guide your way,
To bring you peace and light each day.

So hold it close, both night and day,
And whisper when you need to pray.
You're never ever on your own,
God walks with you; you're never alone.

Parent & Carers Guide

Dear parents and carers, this book is for you,
To help young hearts find what is true.

Parents & Carers Guide

1. Set a Time That Feels Just Right

Choose a time that suits your day,
At morning light or after play.
Bedtime prayers are calm and sweet,
A perfect way to feel complete.
Just six short lines and time to share,
Will grow a heart that learns to care.

2. Let Children Choose a Saint Each Day

Let them decide who they will meet,
With stories strong or soft and sweet.
Saint Michael helps when they feel fear,
Saint Clare brings calm when sleep draws near.
This gives their soul a guiding way,
To talk to saints throughout the day.

Parents & Carers Guide

3. Reflect a Bit, Then Talk It Through

After a prayer, take time to pause,
And ask some questions, just because!
"What words stayed with you, deep in your heart?"
"Did something you hear feel lovely and smart?"
Simple chats with children like seeds will grow,
And help God's love begin to show.

4. Get Creative, Make It Fun!

With colours bright or crafting glue,
There's lots of fun that you can do.
Draw each saint with stars and skies,
Or act their stories bold and wise.
Build small altars with delight,
And bring their stories into light.

Parents & Carers Guide

5. Link It to Their Everyday

When life feels hard or they feel blue,
A prayer can help them think it through.
Lost a toy or feeling shy?
Speak to Saint Anthony, give it a try.
Link each prayer to what they face,
And help them grow in love and grace.

6. Celebrate the Holy Days

Feast days are a joy to share
With little acts of love and care.
Bake a treat or light a flame,
Say a prayer and speak their name.
It doesn't need to be a fuss,
Just mark the day with faith and trust.

Parents & Carers Guide

7. A Final Thought to Hold in Heart

You don't need plans that must be tight
Just moments filled with love and light.
This book's a friend to guide the way,
With saintly help for every day.
Let wonder bloom, let kindness grow,
And trust God walks with those you know.

What is Prayer?

Prayer is a way to share your day,
The saints love to hear what you have to say.

What is Prayer?

What is a prayer? It's more than a word,
It's how our small voices are lovingly heard.
It's talking to God with a whisper or shout,
Telling Him our worries, our joys, and our doubts.

Prayer can be quiet, or loud like a song,
It can happen at school, or when things go wrong.
It's there in the morning, at bedtime too
God listens, always, to me and to you.

And when we pray, we're never alone,
The saints in Heaven are in God's home.
They once lived on Earth, just like we do,
They trusted in God and always stayed tru

What is Prayer?

Some were gentle, and some were bold,
Some were young, and some were old.
Each one followed God's loving way,
And now they help us when we pray.

When you're happy, or sad, or feeling unsure,
A saint can help your spirit soar.
They each have gifts, unique and bright,
To guide you with their special light.

Do you feel scared? Or full of delight?
Are your thoughts too busy late at night?
Do you want to help the ones you love?
Or send good wishes to God above?

What is Prayer?

This book is your space to sit and be still,
To calm your heart, to shape your will.
Each saint is ready to hear your call,
Their love and strength can help us all.

So come meet these saints, both brave and kind,
They'll guide your heart, and soul and mind.
With open hands and a heart that's true,
Say a little prayer, God's waiting for you!

The Saints

Get to know twenty special saints,
With kind big hearts and no complaints.

Saint Mary
Mother of Love

When to Pray
When you need comfort, safety, or motherly love

Guardian Of
Women
Families
The World

Mary's Prayer
Dear Mary, shining bright from above,
You held your son and showed him love.
Please hold my hand both day and night,
And teach me how to choose what's right.
When I am scared or feel alone,
Wrap me in love as you did your own.

Saint Joseph
Guardian of Hearts

When to Pray
When you want to help at home, or need strength to do good work

Guardian Of ♡
Fathers
Workers
Families

Joseph's Prayer
Saint Joseph, quiet and full of care,
You built a home with love to share.
Your hands made tables, doors, and dreams,
While kindness flowed in steady streams.
Please help me work with joy each day,
To love my family, learn, and pray.

Saint Francis
Of Assisi - Voice of Creation

When to Pray
When you're outside in nature, with animals, or want to be kind and gentle

Guardian Of
Animals
Nature

Francis's Prayer
Saint Francis, you loved all God made,
From sun and stars to leafy shade.
You talked to birds and calmed the beasts,
And shared your food in every feast.
Please help me care for the Earth and air,
And treat all life with love and care.

Saint Therese
Of Lisieux - The Little Flower

When to Pray
When you want to do something kind or feel too small to make a difference

Guardian Of
Florists
Missions
Children

Therese's Prayer
Dear Saint Therese, so sweet yet strong,
You showed God's love to one and all.
With flowers and smiles, your kindness grew,
In every little thing you'd do.
Teach me to notice small chances to care,
And spread God's love like petals in air.

Saint Michael
Defender of Light

When to Pray
When you're afraid, need protection, or face something scary

Guardian Of
Protection
Soldiers
Police

Michael's Prayer
Saint Michael, mighty, fierce, and fast,
You guard God's children, first to last.
When shadows creep or loud fears shout,
Your shining sword will cast them out.
With shield and sword, help me to stand,
And walk each day with God's own hand.

Saint Clare

Light in the Darkness

When to Pray
At bedtime, during quiet time, or when your mind feels busy and you need to relax.

Guardian Of
A good nights sleep
Eye issues
Good Weather

Clare's Prayer
Saint Clare, watch over me through the night,
And wrap me in your gentle light.
Please calm my thoughts and help me rest,
With God's sweet love inside my chest.
Keep watch beside me as I sleep,
And let my heart find rest thats deep.

Saint Nicholas
The Gentle Giver

When to Pray
When giving or receiving, or when you want to be kind to others

Guardian Of
Children
Sailors
Generosity

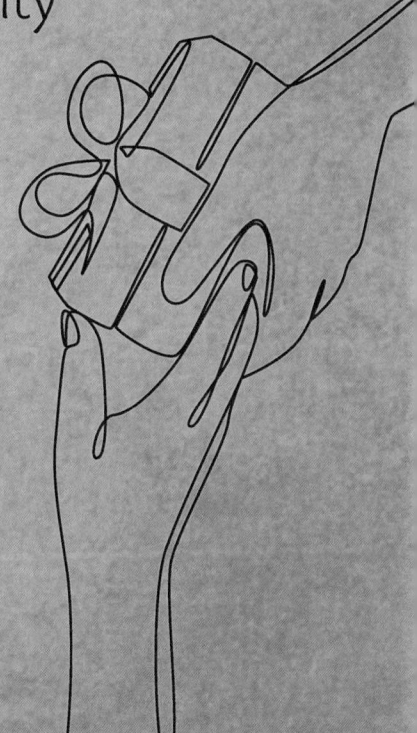

Nicholas's Prayer
Saint Nicholas, so kind and good,
You helped the poor with gifts and food.
You gave in secret, late at night,
To fill sad hearts with joy and light.
I'll grow how I give and care,
And help spread kindness everywhere.

Saint Anthony

Of Padua - Seeker of the Lost

When to Pray
When you've lost something or feel confused

Guardian Of
Lost things
Travellers
The poor

Anthony's Prayer
Saint Anthony, so clever and wise,
You help us see with our own eyes.
When things are lost or out of view,
Please help me find what's right and true.
And more than things, please help me find,
God's gentle peace within my mind.

Saint Patrick

Voice of the Shepherd

When to Pray
When learning about God, trying to teach others about Jesus or be true to your faith.

Guardian Of
Engineers
Teachers
Those scared of snakes

Patrick's Prayer
Saint Patrick, brave and full of cheer,
You taught God's love both far and near.
You spoke of Father, Spirit, Son,
And taught the world they all are one.
Walk with me as I learn each day,
To share God's love in my own way.

Saint Mark

Messenger of Grace

When to Pray
When writing or reading, or learning to write and read, especially about faith

Guardian Of
Lions
Lawyers
Venice

Mark's Prayer
Saint Mark, you told of Jesus' care,
In words so clear, the world could share.
Help me to tell His story too,
With crayons, songs, or something new.
Sit beside me when I'm shy to speak,
And give my voice the courage I seek.

Saint Luke
Healer of Hearts

When to Pray
When someone is sick or you want to be caring and kind

Guardian Of
Doctors
Artists
Students

Luke's Prayer
Saint Luke, with gentle healer's hands,
You cared for hearts in many lands.
Help me to notice hurt and need,
And act with love in thought and deed.
Let kindness grow in all I do,
So others feel God's healing too.

Saint George
The Brave Knight

When to Pray
When you feel scared or need courage to do something brave

Guardian Of
Soldiers
Scouts
Courage

George's Prayer
Saint George, so fearless, bold, and bright,
You battled wrong and stood for right.
Please help me face what makes me scared,
With trust I'll be strong and prepared.
Let me be brave, and kind and true,
And stand for good in all I do.

Saint Charbel
The Miracle Monk

When to Pray
When you need strength, healing, or want to be closer to Jesus through prayer

Guardian Of
Lebanon
Miracles
Those who suffer quietly

Charbel's Prayer
Saint Charbel, quiet, pure, and wise,
You prayed beneath the mountain skies.
Though you were hidden from the crowd,
Your faith in God was strong and proud.
Please teach my heart to seek his face,
In silent prayer and peaceful grace.

Saint Ephrem
Poet of Light

When to Pray
When writing, creating, or learning more about God

Guardian Of
Spiritual writers,
Poets,
Deacons

Ephrem's Prayer
Saint Ephrem, poet filled with grace,
You sang of God in every place.
Your words were bright, your hymns divine,
A shining truth in every line.
Help me to write and learn with care,
And lift my thoughts in holy prayer.

Saint Gregory
The Illuminator

When to Pray
When you need hope or are sharing your faith

Guardian Of
Armenia,
Christian conversion,
Hope in hard times.

Gregory's Prayer
Saint Gregory, your faith stood tall,
You answered God's most daring call.
You lit a fire that burned so bright,
And turned a nation toward the Light.
Help me be brave and speak God's name,
And shine with love, not seek out fame.

Saint Isaac

Of Nineveh - Voice of Mercy

When to Pray
When you need patience or want to forgive others

Guardian Of
Forgiveness, Spiritual growth, Compassion.

Isaac's Prayer

Saint Isaac, calm and full of peace,
You showed us how our fears can cease.
You taught that mercy makes us whole,
And brings God's healing to the soul.
Help me forgive and understand,
And share God's love with open hands.

Saint Josephine

Bakhitan - Heart Full of Grace

When to Pray
When you're feeling hurt, need help forgiving someone, or want to feel peace.

Guardian Of
Sudan,
People in need of forgiveness,
Those who are suffering.

Josephine's Prayer
Saint Josephine, so calm and free,
You showed what true faith needs to be.
Though life was hard, you chose to shine,
With hope and peace that felt divine.
Please help me when I'm feeling sad,
To trust in God and not stay mad.

Saint Rose

Of Lima - Garden of Grace

When to Pray

When you want to grow in patience, or show love through acts of kindness

Guardian Of

South America, Florists, Gardeners.

Rose's Prayer

Saint Rose, so gentle, strong, and fair,
You found God's joy in humble care.
You knelt with flowers at Jesus' feet,
And shared His love with all you'd meet.
Plant in me seeds of patience and cheer,
So kindness can bloom all through the year.

Saint Bridget
Star of the North

When to Pray
When you're traveling, need guidance, or want to listen to God's voice in quiet prayer.

Guardian Of
Sweden, Widows, Travelers.

Bridget's Prayer
Saint Bridget, traveler, wise and bright,
You followed God with heart and sight.
Your dreams were filled with Heaven's call,
You shared His love and gave your all.
Guide my thoughts both near and far,
To follow Jesus like a star.

Saint Mary Mckillop
Teacher of Hope

When to Pray
when you're learning something new, helping others understand, or need courage to do what's right.

Guardian Of
Teachers
The poor
Rural communities

Mary's Prayer
Saint Mary, kind and strong and wise,
You saw the world through caring eyes.
You taught the poor with joyful grace,
And showed God's love in every place.
Please help me share, be brave and true,
And shine with love in all I do.

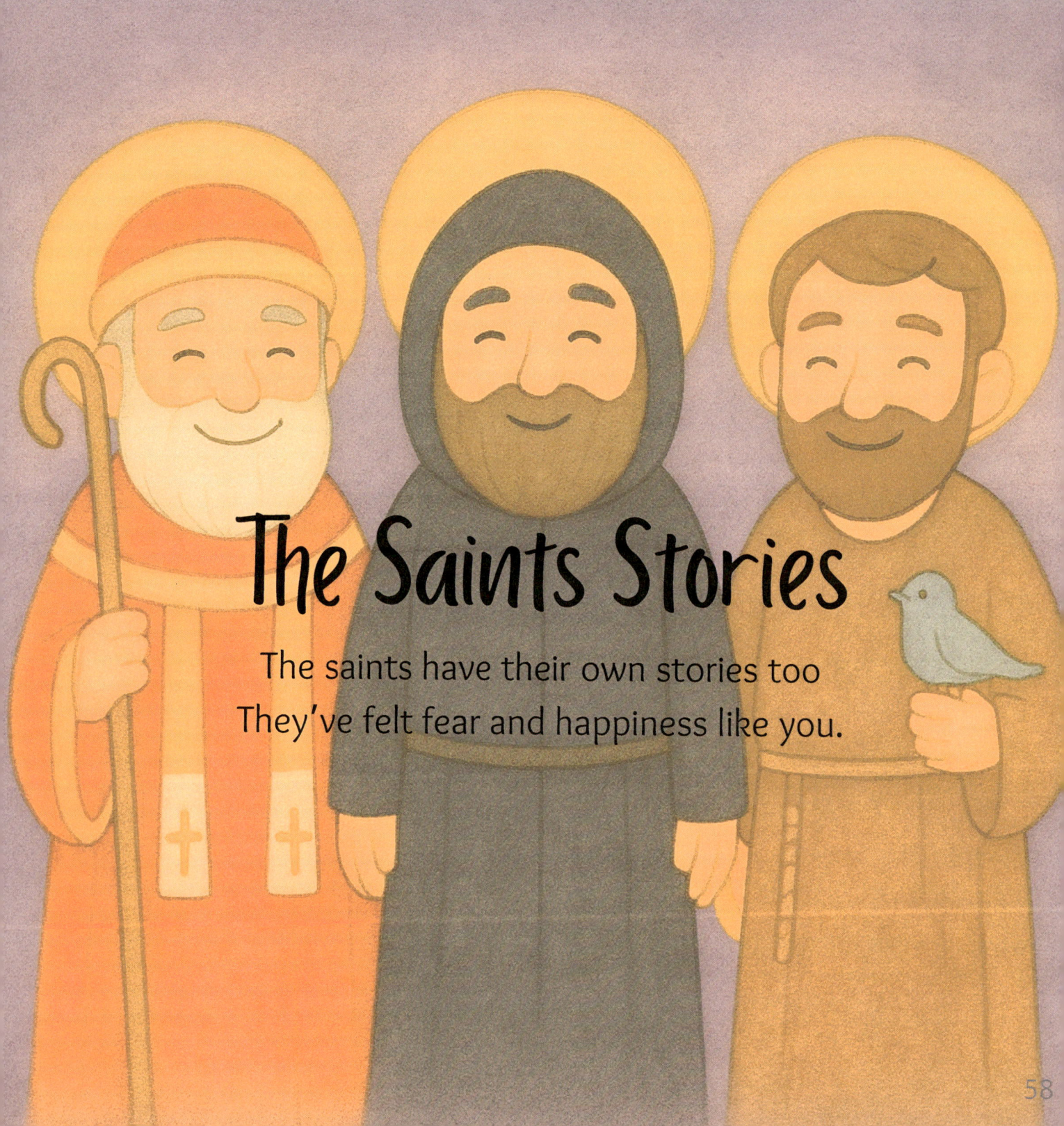

The Saints Stories

The saints have their own stories too
They've felt fear and happiness like you.

Saint Mary (Mother of God)

Saint Mary, the Mother of God, is loved as the mother of Jesus Christ. Her life of faith, gentleness, and motherly care made her a model for all people. Christians turn to her for comfort, guidance, and protection.

Saint Joseph

Saint Joseph, the earthly father of Jesus and husband of Mary, is known for his quiet strength, devotion, and humility. He protected the Holy Family and worked as a carpenter, making him the patron of workers and fathers.

Saint Francis

Saint Francis of Assisi founded the Franciscan Order and is known for his love of animals, nature, and the poor. He gave up a life of wealth to serve God and preach peace, humility, and simplicity.

Saint Therese

Known as the Little Flower, Saint Therese of Lisieux followed a 'little way' of simple acts done with great love. Her short life was filled with deep spiritual wisdom, inspiring many with her gentle faith.

Saint Michael

Saint Michael is the leader of the heavenly armies who defends against evil. Often depicted in armor, he is a symbol of protection and spiritual warfare, and is called upon in times of fear or danger.

Saint Clare

Saint Clare was a follower of Saint Francis and the founder of the Poor Clare's. She lived a life of poverty and devotion, and is remembered for her deep faith and the miraculous light that filled her room during prayer.

Saint Nicholas

Saint Nicholas was a bishop known for secret acts of generosity, especially to children and the poor. His loving spirit of giving inspired the figure of Santa Claus and he is remembered for his charity and kindness.

Saint Anthony

Saint Anthony was a Franciscan priest known for his powerful preaching and help in finding lost items. He is also remembered for his deep knowledge of Scripture and his compassion for the poor.

Saint Patrick

Saint Patrick was a missionary bishop who brought Christianity to Ireland. Known for using a shamrock to explain the Trinity, he faced hardships with courage and converted a nation through faith and perseverance.

Saint Mark

Saint Mark was one of the Gospel writers and a companion of Saint Peter. He is known for his contributions to the early Church and for spreading the message of Christ through his writing and missionary work.

Saint Luke

Saint Luke, author of the Gospel of Luke and the Acts of the Apostles, was a physician and artist. His writings focus on compassion, healing, and the role of the Holy Spirit in the life of the Church.l.

Saint George

Saint George was a Roman soldier and martyr known for his courage and the legendary tale of slaying a dragon. He is a symbol of bravery, standing firm in faith against fear and evil.

Saint Charbel

Saint Charbel Makhlouf was a Maronite monk from Lebanon who lived as a hermit. His deep prayer life and miraculous healings have made him a beloved saint throughout the Christian world.

Saint Ephram

Saint Ephrem the Syrian was a deacon and hymn writer whose poetic works earned him the title 'Harp of the Holy Spirit.' He used beauty, music, and prayer to teach and inspire Christian faith.

Saint Gregory

Saint Gregory converted Armenia to Christianity, making it the first Christian nation. He is revered for his courage, leadership, and missionary zeal during a time of great persecution.

Saint Isaac

Saint Isaac was a 7th-century monk and theologian known for his teachings on compassion, forgiveness, and divine love. He is especially respected in Eastern Christianity for his wisdom and gentle spirit.

Saint Josephine Bakhita

Saint Josephine Bakhita was born in Sudan and endured slavery before finding freedom and faith. She became a nun in Italy and is remembered for her profound forgiveness and joyful trust in God.

Saint Rose

Saint Rose of Lima was the first canonized saint of the Americas. Known for her life of penance, charity, and mystical prayer, she devoted herself to caring for the poor and the sick in Peru.

Saint Bridget

Saint Bridget was a mystic and founder of the Bridgettine Order. Her visions and writings influenced spiritual life in Europe, and she is admired for her deep prayer and bold witness to the truth.

Saint Mary MacKillop

Saint Mary MacKillop was Australias first canonized saint. She co-founded the Sisters of Saint Joseph to provide education for poor and rural children. Her faith, courage, and compassion left a lasting legacy.

Seeking Saintly Guidance

Happy or sad, confused or shy,
A saint can help your spirit fly.

Seeking Saintly Guidance

🕊️ **When You Need Peace, Comfort, or Sleep**
- Saint Mary — 18
- Saint Clare — 28
- Saint Isaac of Nineveh — 48
- Saint Josephine Bakhita — 50
- Saint Bridget of Sweden — 54
- Saint Charbel — 42

 **When You Need Courage, Protection, or Strength**
- Saint Joseph — 20
- Saint Michael the Archangel — 26
- Saint George — 40
- Saint Gregory the Illuminator — 46

Seeking Saintly Guidance

👼 **When You're Feeling Happy, Thankful, or Joyful**
- Saint Therese of Lisieux — 24
- Saint Rose of Lima — 52
- Saint Mark — 36
- Saint Ephrem the Syrian — 44

 **When You're Feeling Lost, Confused, & Need Direction**
- Saint Anthony of Padua — 32
- Saint Luke — 38
- Saint Bridget of Sweden — 54
- Saint Isaac of Nineveh — 48

Seeking Saintly Guidance

💛 **When You Want to Give, Help, or Be Kind**
- Saint Nicholas — 30
- Saint Joseph — 20
- Saint Anthony — 32
- Saint Francis of Assisi — 22

📖 **When You're Learning, Reading, or Creating**
- Saint Mark — 36
- Saint Luke — 38
- Saint Ephrem the Syrian — 44
- Saint Gregory the Illuminator — 46
- Saint Mary MacKillop — 56
- Saint Patrick — 34

Feast Days

Bake a treat or light a flame,
And say a prayer in their sweet name!

Feast Days

Saint Mary (Mother of God)..................Jan-01
Saint Joseph...Mar-19
Saint Francis of Assisi..........................Oct-04
Saint Therese of Lisieux.......................Oct-01
Saint Michael the Archangel................Sep-29
Saint Clare..Aug-11
Saint Nicholas.......................................Dec-06
Saint Anthony of Padua.......................Jun-13
Saint Patrick...Mar-17
Saint Mark..Apr-25
Saint Luke...Oct-18
Saint George..Apr-23
Saint Charbel.......................................Jul-24
Saint Ephrem.......................................June 9
Saint Gregory the Illuminator..............Sep-30
Saint Isaac of Nineveh.........................Jan-28
Saint Josephine Bakhita......................Feb-08
Saint Rose of Lima...............................Aug-23
Saint Bridget of Sweden......................Jul-23
Saint Mary MacKillop...........................Aug-08

A Final Message

Carry these prayers within your heart,
Your saintly friends will do their part.

A Final Message

Dear child, so loved by God above,
   You're wrapped each day in endless love.
   When skies feel dark or hearts feel small,
Just say a prayer, God hears it all.

The saints are near, they know your name,
   They followed God and praised His name
   They'll guide you gently on your way,
   And stay beside you night and day.

Be strong, be kind, be brave and true,
   God's light is always part of you.
   So hold this book and feel God's care,
   Your saintly friends are always there.

www.ingramcontent.com/pod-product-compliance
Lightning Source LLC
Chambersburg PA
CBRC091504220426
43661CB00022B/1309